Away in a Suitcase

A (Twenty) First Century Nativity

by

Fay Rowland

Copyright

© Fay Rowland 2022

The right of Fay Rowland to be identified as the author of this work is asserted in accordance with the Copyright, Designs and Patents Act, 1988.

All rights reserved.

No part of this publication may be reproduced, stored in or introduced into a retrieval system, or transmitted in any form, or by any means (electronic, mechanical, photocopying, recording or otherwise) without the prior written permission of the author.

Visit the author's website at www.fayrowland.co.uk

Typeset by Attic Studios, England
in Century Gothic

Published by Thomas Salt Books

ISBN: 9781915150103

Using This Script

Permission is hereby granted to the owner to make up to 30 copies of this script for rehearsal and performance in educational and faith settings. You must not sell the copies and they must be destroyed after use.

If you do not own this book, you may not copy it.

If you make a recording of your performance, you may place the video on a non-commercial personal, church, or school website or video channel. You must include the following copyright notice at the end of your video.

Script by Fay Rowland
© copyright Fay Rowland 2022
All rights reserved. Used by permission
For further information visit www.reflectionary.org

If you wish to use this script for any commercial purpose, please contact the author (fay@fayrowland.co.uk).

Images © copyright by Revd Ally Barrett. Please visit *reverendally.org* for more artwork, hymns and poems, and for permission to use.

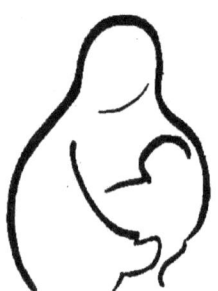

Amazon reviews for 'God Is With Us – Everywhere!'

★★★★★ Phoebe

Totally recommend this easy to use, funny Nativity play

What an incredible gift this was for a Christmas during the coronavirus pandemic!

It is funny, easy to use and has quite a few small parts, which is great to get folks of all ages across the congregation involved. The parts were easily recorded separately and put together as a video.

We even managed to get the Moderator of the General Assembly of the Church of Scotland to play one of the wise men!

Fantastic resource and talented, helpful writer.

★★★★★ Katie

Excellent Nativity Script

Performed this online via video recordings - everyone loved it. A great, meaningful script, beautifully written. Funny in places and very moving.

★★★★★ Mrs K L Holt

Brilliant

This is brilliant. What an amazing alternative and fun way of telling the wonderful story of Jesus' birth and reminding us of how God is with us in all things.

Acknowledgements

My grateful thanks, as always, to my children for putting up with a mum who is always going 'tappity, tappity, tap' on the keyboard and forcing them to eat pizza for tea. (Not sure that they mind, really.)

Thanks also to my venerable alpha-reader, Steve D, and to all those who have given constructive criticism on this and other projects.

Enormous thanks to Ally for her wonderful artwork. You'll find snippets of her work on the cover and scattered around, ensuring that the sections start on the correct-facing pages and beautifying what would otherwise be blank spaces.

Thank you, finally, to those who support my writing ministry at The Reflectionary. The resources there are given away for free because I believe this stuff is important, but I do still need to make a living! If you have not visited yet, may I encourage you to pop along to www.reflectionary.org?

By buying this book you are helping me to continue so, for being part of the team, gentle reader, THANK YOU! You're a star!

(That's always assuming you've actually bought this book. If you haven't, why not?)

Away in a Suitcase

A (Twenty) First Century Nativity

Away in a Suitcase

is a funny, festive yet poignant re-telling of the Nativity story set in modern times, with a charming transformation into a traditional crib scene at the end.

Mary and Joseph find their hotel room has been double-booked by three visiting foreigners, and there are no travel cots left, so they have to use a suitcase as their baby's first bed.

The play has a running time of 20-25 minutes, longer if you add carols between the scenes, and includes a short Christmas message from the narrator or another speaker such as a head teacher or a minister.

There are parts suitable for a range of abilities, with a minimum cast of 19 adjustable to 30 or more.

The costumes are deliberately simple, and there are few props and little scenery. 'Away in a Suitcase' is perfect for your Crib Service, All-Age Worship, Messy Church or school Nativity play.

Cast

There are 11 main speaking parts, including a Narrator and all the traditional characters. These are best suited to more-confident actors.

For those who are less confident, there are choruses of Hotel Staff and Angels. These act and speak as groups, perfect for those who do not want a main part but want more than walk-ons. Finally, there are optional non-speaking parts for younger children.

Speaking Parts

- **Narr** — Narrator, 'reads' from large Bible
- **Mary** — College student
- **Mum** — Practical and friendly
- **Gabriel** — Cool. Think 'The Fonz'
- **Joe** — Likes computer games
- **Manager** — Ultra-polite and apologetic
- **Amos** — Boss shepherd
- **Laban** — Apprentice shepherd
- **Balthazar** — Wise man
- **Melchior** — Wise man
- **Caspar** — Wise man
- **Postie** — Same person as Mum

Chorus Parts

- **Hotel Staff**   5 to 10 tall people to form 'wall'
- **Angels**   4 to 12 people

Non-Speaking Parts

- **Sheep**   5 to 15 children (optional)

If you need a larger cast, form a choir to lead the carols between scenes. You can also have scene introducers who walk on stage with a large sign and announce each scene. They can join the transformation scene at the end by adding tinsel and surrounding the tableau.

A Note on Angels

When we think of angels in children's nativity plays, most of us imagine cute little girls in pigtails and tinsel.

Angels in the Bible, however, are powerfully masculine. Think of Arnold Schwarzenegger or Dwayne 'The Rock' Johnson. (That's why the first thing angels say is almost always 'Do not be afraid.')

So, while you may choose to cast Gabriel's chorus of angels as small, cute and glittery, Gabriel himself should be tall, confident and cool.

Costumes

Most characters are initially in modern dress and transform into traditional costumes ready for the final reveal. They do this behind a 'wall' made from Hotel Staff and Angels.

Costumes do not have to be complex. Modern dress can be jeans and a hoodie, or a white shirt or t-shirt with school uniform trousers.

You can make simple robes with a blanket draped like a cloak and the ever-present checked tea towel, or you can use supermarket nativity costumes.

If possible, avoid clothing that needs to go over the head because the change into traditional costumes happens on stage. Zip-up hoodies are great because they are easy to take off, and you can hide a whole lot underneath.

Many characters transform into angels for the final reveal. They wear white shirts or t-shirts as part of their modern dress, then remove any outer layer (jacket, apron, etc) and add a lollipop-shaped piece of tinsel. This can be worn as a halo with the tail down the back, or as a tie by placing the loop under a shirt collar. They can hide the tinsel halos/ties in a pocket until needed for the final reveal.

Costume Suggestions (→ transformation)

Narr White shirt, black/grey trousers
→ Add tinsel halo/tie if joining the crib scene

Mary Blue dress tucked up under zip-up hoodie, leggings, cushion & baby
→ Remove hoodie, add blue shawl draped over head, swap cushion for baby

Mum/Postie White shirt, jeans and coloured cardigan
→ Remove cardigan, add cap and parcel to become Postie

Gabriel Leather jacket, white shirt or t-shirt, jeans, big boots, optional wings
→ Remove jacket, add tinsel halo/tie

Joe Robe tucked up under zip-up hoodie, jeans
→ Remove hoodie, add head dress

Manager White shirt, black/grey trousers and jacket
→ Remove jacket, add tinsel halo/tie

Staff White shirt, black/grey trousers, apron
→ Remove apron, add tinsel halo/tie

Shepherds	Robe tucked up under zip-up hoodie, high-vis jacket, jeans
→	Remove hoodie and high-vis, add head dress
Sheep	Sheep costume, or party clothes and holding sheep toy
	(You can have one child dressed as a cow or donkey as a joke for the shepherds)
→	No change
Angels	All in white with tinsel belt, or Christmas jumper, jeans, tinsel halo/tie
→	No change
Wise Men	Robe tucked up under white lab coat
→	Remove lab coat, add optional crown or beard
Postie	White shirt, jeans, cap, parcel
→	Remove cap, add tinsel halo/tie

Props

Large comfy armchair

Free-standing door (optional)

Scene 1 large Bible (Narr) also throughout
textbook (Mary)

Scene 2 VR headset (Joe)
phone (Joe)

Scene 3 cushion (Mary)
letter (Joe)
phone (Joe)

Scene 4 cushion (Mary)
suitcase with clothes (Joe)

Scene 5 2 chairs, two mugs (Amos and Laban)

Scene 6 3 travel bags containing:
Lynx Gold gift set (Bal)
large bottle marked 'Frankincense' (Mel)
large hand cream (Cas)

Scene 7 large parcel containing a phone (Postie)
box or small stool (Gabriel)
Jesus doll (Mary)

Staging

There is a large comfy chair centre stage, not too near the front. There needs to be enough room in front of the chair for the suitcase and two rows of children (which hide the assembling crib scene), and for scenes 5, 6 & 7 to happen in front of that.

Behind the chair is a box or small stool, and a doll wrapped in a pillowcase. The VR headset (safety goggles painted black) is at one side of the chair.

At one side of the stage, towards the front, there is a real or imaginary door to the outside. All characters entering and leaving to the outside go through this door. Other entrances and exits happen at the other side or as convenient.

Stage directions are given *in italics*. Stage directions at the end of a scene happen while the next scenes take place. For example, at the end of scene 4, Mary changes into traditional costume during scenes 5 and 6. You do not wait for her to do this before starting scene 5.

Two sound effects are needed: something falling over, and a knock at the door.

If it is possible, dim the lights at the back of the stage over the crib scene at the end of scene 4, then raise the lights for the final reveal, at the end of scene 7.

Crib Scene

During scenes 4, 5 and 6, a traditional crib scene builds up around the chair. The main characters are hidden behind a wall made of Hotel Staff, Angels and other characters. The wall opens to reveal the crib scene at the end of scene 7.

Assembling the Scene

Mary sits in the chair holding Jesus, and Joseph sits on the chair arm.

Manager places the open suitcase at Mary's feet for the manger.

The Shepherds stand to one side behind the chair, and the Wise Men to the other side, forming an arc.

Gabriel stands in the middle of the arc, directly behind the chair, on a box to give him height.

The Hotel Staff form the wall that hides the crib scene. The Angels form another wall in front of the Staff.

During the message, Hotel Staff transform to more Angels

The Reveal

The walls of Hotel Staff and Angels part to reveal the crib scene.

Angels and Hotel Staff stand or kneel to the left and right, framing the scene.

The sheep enter and sit on the floor at the front.

Mary places Jesus in the suitcase-manger by her feet.

Away in a Suitcase

The Script

Away in a Suitcase

Scene 1 – Mary's House

[**Mary** *enters slowly, reading a textbook, and flops sideways on a large comfy chair, centre stage*]

Narr In the sixth month, God sent the angel Gabriel to Nazareth in Galilee.

[*Knock at the door*]

Mary Muuuuuum! There's someone at the door.

Mum [*Offstage*] Can you answer it, Mary?

Mary I can't. I'm in the middle of college work.

Mum And I'm in the middle of fixing your curtain rail, and if I'm not careful I'll ... ooo, errr, oh dear!

[*Crash sound effect*]

Mary Oops.

Mum I'm OK. I'm OK. Ooh, that's going to have a bruise in the morning.

[*Knock at the door*]

Mary Daaaaaad! There's someone at the door.

Mum Your dad's gone on a park run. You'll have to get it.

Mary [*Getting up*] Oh, I s'pose.

[*Knock at the door*]

Alright, alright, I'm coming. Keep your wig on.

*[**Mary** opens 'door', **Gabriel** steps inside]*

Gabriel Greetings, you who are highly favoured! The Lord is with you.

Mary You what?

Gabriel Greetings, you who are highly favoured! The Lord is with you.

Mary *[Giving him a 'what planet are you on?' look]* R-i-i-i-ght. OK.

Gabriel Hello Mary, I am Gabriel. I have a message for you. From the boss. *[Pointing upwards]*

Mary Gabriel? You mean you're an … How do you know my …? A message from …?
You'd better come in.

[Both move to chair]

Sit down?

Gabriel I think you might need the chair.

Mary Why?

Gabriel You're going to have a baby.

Mary *[Looking coy]* Well yes, probably, some day. But Joe and I only got engaged last month.
We've not even set a date for the wedding yet. We certainly weren't planning on having a baby anytime soon. I'm still at college!

Gabriel This will be God's son, not Joseph's.

Mary *[Sitting down suddenly]* But … but … I mean … well … y'know … ummmmn … how?

Gabriel Oh, *[Waving hands]* Holy Spirit and all that, you know.
You will give birth to a son, and you will name him Jesus. He will be great and will be called the Son of the Most High.

Mary Oh. Right. *[Talking to self, rapidly]* Wow! God's son? I mean, WOW! Why me? It's gob-smacking! It's incredible! How will I cope? *[Continue mumbling to self]*

Gabriel *[Speaking over Mary]* So is that OK then?

Mary What? Oh, yes. Yes, let's do it!
[Talking to self again] Crumbs, God's baby! I wonder if he'll look like me?
What kind of nappies does God's son wear?
[Continue while Gabriel leaves]

Gabriel I'll let myself out, then. Bye.

*[**Gabriel** exits through 'door' and **Mum** enters from other side, wiping hands]*

Mum Who was that, dear?

*[**Mary** walks to Mum, taking textbook]*

Mary You'll never guess, Mum. You'll never guess!

*[**Mary** and **Mum** exit]*

Scene 2 – Mary's House, a week later

Narr Now, Mary was pledged to be married to Joseph.

*[Knock at the door, **Mum** enters and answers door]*

Mum Hello, Joe dear. Come on in. You know Mary's away, staying with her cousin Elizabeth?

*[**Joe** enters, looking cross]*

Joe Yeah, I know she's away. That's why I've come round now. I got this text from her last night.

[Showing phone]
A baby? Did you know about this?

Mum Ah, yes dear. I know it looks bad but don't …

Joe *[Interrupting]* Looks bad? It feels bad! Right here. *[Thumps chest]*
She's broken my heart, that girl. Told me some rubbish about an angel visiting her.
Does she think I'm an idiot?

Mum No, Joe, not at all. She loves you. Come and sit down, dear.

Joe Loves me? Well, she's got a funny way of showing it! The wedding's off. *[Flops in chair]*
I've only come round to bring back her CDs.

Mum Now don't be hasty, dear.
Let me get you a cup of tea and you can have a go with that Minebox Playtendo game that you like so much.

*[**Mum** exits and changes character to **Postie**]*

Joe Yeah, OK then. Thanks.

[Puts on VR headset and starts miming]
What was I playing? Oh yes, Aerobatics Ace.

Resume.

Bank left … bank right … deploy ailerons … barrel roll … ah, this is great.

Ooh, thunder cloud ahead!

I'll power up and climb above it.
Raise elevators
[Mimes steep climb]

Wow! The view up here is brilliant.
[Looking round] Great graphics.

*[**Gabriel** enters and walks round Joe]*

Joe *[Watching Gabriel as he walks around]*
Amazing detail! That angel looks so real.
I could almost reach out and touch him.

Gabriel Joseph!

Joe Woo! Great 3D sound too!

Gabriel Joseph! Don't be afraid to take Mary as your wife, because her baby is from the Holy Spirit.

She will give birth to a son, and you will name him Jesus, because he will save his people from their sins.

*[**Joe**'s jaw drops. **Gabriel** exits. Joe watches him in stunned silence]*

Joe   *[Removing headset]*
What just happened there?

[Addressing Mum, offstage]
Er, you know what I said about the wedding? Forget that. It's back on.

And could I have a couple of sugars in my tea, please?

*[**Joe** exits, taking headset]*

Scene 3 – Mary's House, several months later

Narr   In those days Caesar Augustus issued a decree that all people must register …

[**Joe** and **Mary** enter, Joe is reading a letter, Mary is heavily pregnant]

Mary   What's that you're reading, Joe?

Joe   A letter from the Inland Revenue. We have to register Junior's name if we want a tax rebate for him.

Mary   Already? He's not even born yet!
[Flops into chair]

Joe   Yeah, it's a slow process. They've got a backlog as long as the orbit of Jupiter.

Mary   So do we fill in a form, or can we do it online?

Joe   Neither. We have to register in person. They have an open day next week at their office in Bethlehem. We could go to that.

Mary   Do I have to go too?

Joe   Yeah, sorry. They need both of us.
We could make it like a holiday, a mini-break in Bethlehem, call in and visit some of the relatives. You could go shopping or have a spa day with my cousin June. You two get on really well. What do you say?

Mary   I dunno. The baby's nearly due and I feel like a whale on legs.

Joe I'll make it OK. I'll book us a nice hotel and we'll be back before Junior comes along.

Mary Oh, alright then.
Give us a hand up, will you?

[**Joe** and **Mary** struggle to get Mary our of chair]

But somewhere nice, mind. None of your manky Travel Inn Express.

Joe Whatever you say, my sweet.
[Tapping on phone]
Full English breakfast or continental?

[**Joe** and **Mary** exit, Joe still tapping on phone]

Scene 4 – Hotel Bethlehem

Narr So Joseph went to the town of Bethlehem with Mary, who was expecting a baby.

*[**Mary** and **Joe** enter, Joe has a suitcase]*

Joe I'm sorry, Mary, sweetheart. I know you didn't want Travel Inn Express, but everywhere else was booked up solid. And this was their last room.

Mary Joe, I'm so tired after that long journey that all I want is a nice comfy bed.

Joe You relax, dear. I'll get the keys.
[Puts suitcase down, mimes desk bell] PING!

*[**Manager** enters, bowing obsequiously]*

M'ger Good evening sir, madam, and welcome to the Hotel Bethlehem. How may I help you?

Joe Hello. I made a reservation online. Room 25-12. Could we have our keys, please?

M'ger Oh dear. Room 25-12?

Joe Yes. Is there a problem?

M'ger Indeed there is, sir. I do wish sir had rung to confirm. Room 25-12 is unavailable, I'm afraid.

Mary *[Very quiet]* Joe.

Joe What! I booked it last week!

M'ger If sir had read the small print, he would have noted that online reservations expire at 10pm.

	It is now 10:05, sir. And rooms are in great demand.
Mary	[*Quiet*] Joe.
Joe	So you've given our room to someone else?
M'ger	Indeed. Although sir will be pleased to know that his small oversight has provided accommodation to three foreign VIPs, here for an astronomy conference, I gather. They were very happy to find a vacant room in the middle of Bethlehem. Sir is so kind.
Mary	[*Medium loud*] Joe.
Joe	But where are we going to stay? Do you have any other rooms?
M'ger	I'm afraid not, sir. We are like a brand-new library – fully booked. [*Silly laugh*]
Mary	[*Getting louder*] Joe.
Joe	I suppose you don't have … ummmn … like … a stable round the back, or anything, do you?
M'ger	A Stable? Sir is having a laugh. Where do you think this is, Old MacDonald's Farm?
Mary	[*Loud, tugging Joe's sleeve*] Joe!
Joe	[*Finally noticing*] What is it, Mary?
Mary	The baby! It's coming!
Joe	[*Horrified*] What, now?
Mary	Now!

M'ger   Now? Oh, my word! A baby?
[To wings] Staff! Staff!
[To Joe] You can use my office. There's a snack machine and free Wi-Fi.

[Hotel **Staff** hurry on]

[To Hotel Staff]
Take these good people to my office and make them as comfortable as possible.
Break out the emergency pot noodles if you need to.

Staff   [Speaking all together or different lines for different people]
The emergency pot noodles?
Certainly sir!
[To Mary and Joe]
Come this way, please.

[**Mary**, **Joe** and **Staff** move to chair.
Mary sits on chair and **Joe** kneels beside (he will sit on the arm for the big reveal).

Staff form a wall in front of chair, backs to the audience, hiding Mary and Joe.

Manager paces around stage.]

M'ger   Oh dear, oh dear, oh dear! There was nothing about this in the staff training manual.

They'll need baby clothes.
Ummmn ... Oh! A pillowcase will do nicely.
Now what about a bed? All the travel cots are in use.

[Spots Joe's suitcase]
Perfect!
[To Mary and Joe]
Look! You can use this suitcase as a cot for the baby!

*[**Manager** takes suitcase behind the wall and places it open at Mary's feet.*

***Manager** joins wall.*

*While hidden, **Mary** and **Joe** change to traditional clothes.*
***Mary** hides her cushion behind the chair and gets Jesus doll.*

If possible, dim the lights over the crib scene until the reveal at the end of Scene 7.]

Scene 5 – Hillside Hut

Narr And there were shepherds abiding in the fields, keeping watch over their flocks by night.

*[**Amos** and **Laban** enter, each with a chair and mug, and place chairs centre stage, in front of wall of Staff]*

Amos [Sitting] Ah, modern technology. It's great, innit?

Laban [Sitting] Yeah.

Amos I mean, when I was training to be a shepherd, we didn't have none of this tech.
[Indicating imaginary screens in front of them]
None of these closed-circuit TVs and drones and whatnot.
Oh no. We had to watch sheep by actually watching them. Out in the cold, all seated on the ground.

Laban Yeah.

Amos It's so much better these days, sat in our cosy cabin, with a fully-automatic sock washer and endless cups of tea, eh?

Laban Yeah.

*[**Amos** and **Laban** clink mugs]*

Amos Anyway *[Looking at watch]* it's time to count the sheep.

Laban Yeah.

[As Amos names each sheep, a child runs on stage and waves (if dressed as a sheep) or holds up sheep toy, then runs off.

If you do not have children playing sheep, Laban spots each sheep in the audience as Amos names them.

Adjust the number of sheep to suit. Amos can use a list if needed.

If you have one child dressed as a cow/donkey, Amos and Laban are silent and then shrug as the child runs on stage, waves, and runs off.]

Amos   Right, there's
[First sheep runs on stage]
Baatholemew,
Lambert,
Fleeceity,
Bert**ram**,
Ewenice,
Rambo,
Baarbara,
Pet**ewe**nia,
Rameses,
Baatimeaus,
J**ewe**dy,
Ramona,
Al**baa**rt and
Shaun.

Yep, that's the lot.

Time for more tea. Put the kettle on, Laban.
*[**Amos** hands **Laban** his mug]*

Laban   Why do I always make the tea, Amos? It must be your turn.

Amos   *[Pointing to self]* Who's got BTec Certified Shepherding Level Two?
[Pointing to Laban] Who's the apprentice? Make the tea!

[Knock at the door]

Who's that? It's the middle of the night and we're miles from nowhere out here!

*[**Laban** opens the 'door' and stands staring outside with mouth open]*

Amos   Tell 'em to come in quick, they're letting all the heat out. And make sure they wipe their feet. I'm not having muddy wellies all over my nice clean cabin.

Laban   I … I … I don't think they're wearing wellies, Amos. *[Stands back to let Gabriel in]*

*[**Gabriel** strides in]*

Gabriel   *[Loud voice]* Do not be afraid!

Am/Lab   ARGHHHHHH! *[Both run screaming to other side of stage]*

Gabriel   *[To audience]* This always happens.
[To shepherds] Seriously. I'm not going to bite you. Did I hear the kettle?

*[**Amos** opens and closes his mouth like a goldfish, pointing at Gabriel]*

Laban   Er, yes. I was just making tea. Would you like some?

Gabriel   Oh yes. I'm parched. *[Sitting]*

Amos   *[Still looking like a goldfish]* Whaa … whaa … whaa …

Gabriel   *[To Laban, nodding at Amos]* Is he alright?

Laban   He wants to know what you are doing here. We don't get angels knocking on our door every night.

Gabriel   Oh yes. Sorry. Nearly forgot.

[Standing and proclaiming]
Behold, I bring you good news of great joy.
Your Saviour is born today in Bethlehem.
He is Christ, the Lord.

And this is how you will know him: You will find the baby wrapped in a pillowcase and lying in a suitcase.

[Looking puzzled and addressing someone offstage]
Are you sure that's the right line? 'Cos I thought it was … No, it **is** right? … You sure? … OK.

[Proclaiming again]
...and lying in a suitcase!

[Sitting and addressing the door]
Come on in, team!

[**Angels** *enter and stand along front of stage*

if using two groups of angels, number them alternately 1 & 2 across the stage.
All of group 1 speak together, then all of group 2.
Alternatively, all angels speak both lines.]

Narr [*While angels get into place*]
And suddenly, with the angel there was a multitude of the heavenly host, praising God and saying:

Angels 1 [*Raising arms*] Glory to God in the highest heaven!

Angels 2 [*Raising arms*] Peace on earth, and good will to all people!

Laban [*Pause*] Crikey!

Amos [*Pause*] Yeah.

Laban C'mon, let's go and find this baby. What did he say, in a suitcase? Weird!

[**Gabriel** *exits, taking the chairs with him.*

Amos *and* **Laban** *move behind the wall and form half of arc to one side of the chair, kneeling to remain hidden. They change into traditional dress.*

Angels *form a second row of wall, in front of Hotel Staff, backs towards audience]*

Scene 6 – Hotel Bethlehem

Narr   And wise men came from the east saying …

*[**Balthazar**, **Melchior** and **Caspar** enter]*

Bal   … 'where is the one born king of the Jews?'
is the question I would be asking if I didn't have
a much bigger question on my mind.

Mel   What question is that, Balthazar?

Cas   Is it 'Why have we only got one hotel room for
three of us?'

Bal   Er, no, but that is a good question. Who booked
the room?

Bal/Cas   *[Pointing]* MELCHIOR!

Mel   It was all I could get! The other hotels were
booked up solid. I only got this room because
some other guests didn't turn up.

Cas   Oh well, it'll do I suppose. But if it's not the room,
what is Balthazar's question?

Bal   I'm glad you asked, Caspar. *[Striking
'thoughtful' pose]* It is a question that wise men
like us have wrestled with since the dawn of
time.

*[**Bal** gazes into the middle-distance. **Mel** and **Cas** follow his gaze, wondering what he's looking at]*

A question of eternal significance and timeless
consequence.
A question that rivals DNA in complexity, and

exceeds the ability of the human brain to fathom.

Mel/Cas What is the unending question, O wise and knowledgeable one?

Bal Where on earth is our luggage?

Mel Our luggage?

Cas Are you saying that the airline lost our bags? Again?

Bal Yes! It's a complete disaster, a total nightmare, a catastrophe, a tragedy, a cataclysm, a …

Mel *[Interrupting]* Calm down, Balthazar! Losing our luggage is not that bad.

Cas Yes. We can always buy more socks tomorrow.

Bal It's not the socks, boys. Haven't you realised?

*[**Mel** and **Cas** look blank]*

The gifts?

*[**Mel** and **Cas** look blank]*

For the new baby king?

*[**Mel** and **Cas** look blank]*

All *[Realising]* They're in the suitcases!

Bal What are we going to do? We can't turn up empty-handed. He'll think we're a right bunch of cheapskates.

Mel Maybe we've got something in our hand luggage.

Cas For a baby? I don't think I packed a teddy bear in my carry-on.

Bal The original gifts weren't exactly child-friendly. These can't be any worse.
[Rummaging]
I've got this shower gel and shaving foam set.
[Shows Lynx Gold]

[**Mel** and **Cas** give him a questioning look, miming shaving]

Bal He'll ... grow into it?

Mel [Rummaging]
I got this for my mum from the duty free.
[Shows large perfume bottle, mimics advert with heavy French accent]
Frankincense, eau de parfam, pour homme, pour femme, pour vous.

[**Bal** and **Cas** look at each other and shrug]

Cas Yeah, right.
[Rummaging] Here's something a bit more practical.
[Shows bottle of hand cream]
Moisturising hand cream [Reading label] with aloe vera and myrrh. Perfect for the royal botty. Don't want him getting nappy rash now, do we?

Bal Good, that's all settled. Now, it's getting late. We should try to find the baby.
I'll ring down to the front desk and ask the manager if he knows anything.
[Mimes using phone]

> Hello? Yes, it's the three gents in room 25-12. Would you happen to know anything about a new baby?
> *[Listens]* ... Yes, that's right. A new baby. Born this night. In Bethlehem.
> *[Listens]* ... You do? *[To others]* He does!

*[**Mel** and **Car** cheer]*

> He's in this hotel? *[To others]* He's in this hotel!

*[**Mel** and **Car** cheer]*

> Mmhhm, mmhhm. OK, thanks. Bye.
> *[Puts 'phone' down]*

Mel   Well?

Cas   Where is he?

Bal   He's in the manager's office. It's just off the lobby, downstairs. You remember when we came in, there was that large, spiky lampshade? The manager's office is right underneath that.

Mel   So you mean we ...

Cas   ... just have to ...

All   ... follow the star!

*[**Bal**, **Mel** and **Cas** move behind the wall and form other half of arc to the side of the chair, kneeling to remain hidden. They change into traditional costume.]*

Scene 7 – Right Here, Right Now

[During the message, Hotel **Staff** remove aprons and add tinsel halos/ties to become more **Angels**.

All other characters remove jackets, hoodies etc and get ready for the big reveal.

The message can be delivered by
the **Narrator** (use first section),
or by a different **Speaker** (use second section)

Keep lights dim over crib scene if possible, or have **Narrator/Speaker** move away to one side so that people don't notice cast changing]

If Narrator is giving message

Narr   And it came to pass that there was delivered upon that night the greatest gift of all time.

[**Postie** enters with large parcel]

Postie   Delivery!

Narr   [Taking parcel] Thanks.

Postie   Sign here.

[**Postie** offers hand, **Narr** signs hand]

Postie   Careful, it's fragile.

[**Postie** joins Hotel Staff in wall and changes costume]

Narr   Oh, I'll be careful …

If Speaker is giving message

Narr   And it came to pass that there was delivered upon that night the greatest gift of all time.

[**Postie** enters with large parcel]

Postie   Delivery for [Name of speaker]!

Speaker [Taking parcel] Thanks.

Postie   Sign here.

[**Postie** offers hand, **Speaker** signs hand]

Postie   Careful, it's fragile.

[**Postie** and **Narr** join Hotel Staff in wall and change costume]

Speaker Oh, I'll be careful …

Christmas Message

Oh, I'll be careful, don't you worry. I've been waiting for this for such a long time.

[Carefully opening box]
This is the one that we all have been expecting. The promised one. The one spoken of from ages past. The one who changes everything. The greatest gift of all time.

[Gently takes out and cradles new phone]
Isn't he lovely?
[Talking to phone like a baby]
Yes, you are. You're so lovely. Who's the best phone in the world? You are!

[Noticing audience]
What? Isn't this the great gift of all time?

Maybe you're right. I mean, Christmas presents are great (Ta very much for the phone, Mum) but in a few months they'll bring out a new model and this one won't be so trendy any more.

And the food at Christmas is great, all the roast potatoes and fancy nibbles, but come the day after Boxing Day we're all sick of it.

And the glitz and glitter of Christmas, I love it! I love the decorated trees and the lights and the Christmas films on the telly, but it won't be long before we clear it away and go back to real life.

There's lots about Christmas that is great, but it doesn't last. When the holiday ends and we're back at work, back at school, will it have made any difference? Is a few days of over-eating and wearing novelty jumpers all there is?

This play has told us about the most famous birthday on earth, and we watch it once a year then pack it away in a box marked 'Cute Stuff for Kids', or 'Ancient Myths and Legends'.

Is that all it is? Sure, it happened a long time ago, but this isn't a fairy tale. Even the Roman historians agree that Jesus was a real person.

So what if …

What if this isn't just a cute story for kids? Does it make a difference that this baby grew up and told me to love my enemies and forgive people who don't deserve it? That's really hard. I can't say that I manage it.

But what if ...

What if God is not Santa, and life is not about being on the naughty list or nice list?

The Bible says that none of us are good enough to be on the nice list, and God knows that, so there's no point pretending.

But God doesn't leave us on the naughty list; he does something to fix it. God sent Jesus to move us to the nice list because Jesus **is** good enough.

So what if ...

What if this first-century story still happens today, in the twenty-first-century? I wonder who I would be in the scene: a not-so-wise man perhaps, or the hotel waiter who brought the pot noodle. I wonder who you would be.

This Christmas, I wonder where we will meet Jesus, God with us, born as the child who changes everything.

[Turns to watch as crib scene is revealed]

Revealing the Transformation

If lights have been dimmed, raise them now.

Gabriel *walks to centre stage with jacket over shoulder.*

Gabriel *gives his jacket to* **Narr/Speaker** *and adds tinsel halo/tie in view of audience.*

Gabriel *walks behind wall and stands on box behind chair. He should be clearly visible.*

Gabriel *lifts his arms*

(The next items all happen at once)

>*Play intro to 'Silent Night'*

>**Gabriel** *slowly opens arms wide.*

>**Wise Men** *and* **Shepherds** *stand.* **Joe** *sits on arm of chair.*

>*As Gabriel opens his arms,* **Angels** *(inc* **Staff***,* **Manager** *etc) part and move to sides to reveal the crib scene.*

Angels *turn faces toward crib scene and hold out arms across body towards suitcase.*

Sheep *enter and sit around suitcase.*

All *watch as* **Mary** *places Jesus in the suitcase at her feet.*

All *sing first verse of 'Silent Night'.*

About the Author

Hi, I'm Fay.

In no particular order, I am a mum, choc-o-holic, mathematician, author, blogger, knitter, children's worker and mad scientist.

I write The Reflectionary, a weekly blog of original resources for churches, youth groups, children's work and schools' ministry.

Everything is free, so pop along and help yourself at www.reflectionary.org. You can sign up there to have the posts sent straight to your mailbox. No spam ever, I promise!

I studied Theology at Spurgeon's College and at Wesley House, Cambridge, specialising in children's spirituality, and I'm a trainee Lay Minister in the Church of England. You can find links to my published academic works at www.fayrowland.co.uk.

When not writing or studying, I teach maths for a living and spend most of the rest of the time being creative. I worship at a large Anglican church in the English Midlands, where I'm part of the teams for all-age worship and Messy Church.

I live with my children and pet dragon in an untidy house full of noise and glue sticks and mess (which I blame on the kids, but really, it's me).

Other Publications

| A Bucketful of Ideas for Church Drama (the green one)

"Parables as Jesus would have told them – witty and thought-provoking."

#1 Best-Seller in Puppet Scripts!

"Thirty Pieces of Chocolate is a fine pun-run."

Amazon chart-topper.

A(nother) Bucketful of Ideas for Church Drama (the blue one)

14 scripts including CRISP-tingle, a pop-up nativity, and lots more.

"Delivers the timeless truths of scripture in a modern and punchy manner."

God Is With Us – Everywhere!

Featuring a cool Gabriel, terrified shepherds and three confused scientists, this witty yet poignant Nativity is perfect for your school or church production.

"Thank you for your script, we had it at our online carol service yesterday - and it went down a storm!"

#1 Best-Seller in Christian Youth Ministry!

Walking to Bethlehem

25 imaginative devotions for adults and children, with reflective colouring and craft ideas.

"Travel from BC to AD to focus your mind on the road to Bethlehem. Fun and devotional, practical and creative."

#1 Best-Seller in Advent Devotions!

The Big Story

Discover the Bible as one big story of God and God's people, from the very beginning of everything up to the wonder of Easter.

Perfect for personal devotions, for weekly Bible studies and youth groups, discover The Big Story today.

Broken Bits & Weirdness

Meet nine of the Bible's dismal failures and learn how God still loves them (and us), even with our Broken Bits & Weirdness.

With Bible notes, crafts, cooking, colouring and other resources, and studies for Good Friday and Easter Day, this is perfect for Lent or any time of year.

#1 Best-Seller in Bible Meditations!

Creativity Matters

Join thirteen authors as they share their passion for why you should write in their genre and find your own passion as you read.

In my chapter, 'Why Write Drama?', you can discover what makes drama sparkle, and why you shouldn't take your gran to see a Greek satyr play!

URC Prayer Handbooks

I have been a commissioned author for the URC's prayer handbooks for several years.

They are full of original, passionate, quirky and relevant prayers, with each Sunday having several prayers linked to readings from the Revised Common Lectionary. They are suitable for both congregational and private use, using contemporary language and covering a broad range of topics.

Available from the URC's website shop.

www.ingramcontent.com/pod-product-compliance
Lightning Source LLC
Chambersburg PA
CBHW070338120526
44590CB00017B/2932